Uncle Mac's Barbershop

A Lesson About Bullying

Written by
Tina Figueroa

Illustrated by
Erica Fung

AuthorHouse™
1663 Liberty Drive
Bloomington, IN 47403
www.authorhouse.com
Phone: 833-262-8899

This book is printed on acid-free paper.

ISBN: 978-1-6655-5256-1 (sc)
ISBN: 978-1-6655-5255-4 (hc)
ISBN: 978-1-6655-5257-8 (e)

Print information available on the last page.

Published by AuthorHouse 03/23/2022

authorHOUSE®

To my two beautiful grandchildren, Alanah and Di'Milo. I am so blessed to be here to watch you grow up and learn how to respect others while being kind and also speaking up for yourself when you do not receive respect. This will be a challenging task throughout your entire life, but don't let other people's negative attitudes affect your positive attitude. You will experience life's short lessons, but always believe in yourself and God too. You inspired me to write this book .

Love,
Grandma T. T.

I want to acknowledge and thank my son and daughter, Christian "MACnificent Cutz" Lester and Josalynn "Angelicfeaturesbyjos" Davis. You have stood by me through four degrees and now published work. Though we missed quite a few family meetings (you too, Latrina Mullins), we are still standing strong together. Mama would be proud of us. Thank you for your support throughout this journey. I am also grateful to my dream team, who endorsed my published book: long time friends Dr. Fredonia Bean, Dameisha Donald, Angela Harris, and my cousin Jacqueline Mullins. A special thank- you to my loving sister Theresa Barclay. Your professional comments and guidance truly made a difference in my finished work. I am blessed to have all of you in my life.

Tina Figueroa has a PhD in Special Education Leadership. She lives in Baltimore, Maryland, and has been in education for more than twenty-five years. She has spent her career dedicated to children and adults with special needs as a special education teacher, school principal, and special education coordinator in Arkansas, Tennessee, New Jersey, and Maryland. While in Memphis, Tennessee, she founded the Diligent Individuals with Vivid Aspirations (DIVA) program, which targeted at-risk teen girls by supporting their academic, social, and emotional needs. She published an article in the *Rural Special Education Quarterly Journal* in summer of 2003— "I'm Back! Developing a Transition Plan for Students with Disabilities Who Return to Rural School Districts from Mental Health Treatment Facilities." She grew up as a child who attended church, where the Golden Rule was always instilled in her and her siblings.

"Wake up, Milo; we're going to the barbershop today."

"Oh, Dad,, but I don't want to get my hair cut; I look cool like this. Every time I get my hair cut, the kids at school ask silly questions like, ' Hey, Milo, did you get a new haircut? I nod my head and say, ' No, I woke up like this!'"

"Pancakes are ready; come and get them!" Mom yelled from the kitchen.

"Yes, I love pancakes. Pancakes, pancakes, I love pancakes," said Milo.

Honey, eat your breakfast so you can be the first one in your Uncle Mac's barbershop."

"But, Mom, don't I look great like this?"

Mom smiled. "Yes, pumpkin, but just when I think you couldn't look more handsome, you always do after a new haircut."

"OK, OK, I guess you're right," replied Milo.

"Hi, Uncle Mac."

"What's up, shorty? What you got for me?" replied Uncle Mac.

"I brought you myself and my magnificent swag. Did you miss me, Uncle?" replied Milo.

"Yes, I did; I always do, shorty. I picked out a jazzy haircut for you that'll make all the kids in school want to look like you."

"That's great, Uncle Mac! I can't wait to see it."

4

TA-DA!
MACnificent Cutz!

"Ta-da, MACnificent Cutz! How do you like that, shorty?" said Uncle Mac.

"Oh, wow! I love it. I love football. I watch football with my dad all the time. This haircut is incredible. Thanks, Uncle Mac. Put it on my tab."

"Of course, shorty. Bye for now."

6

"Hey, Milo, did you get a new haircut?"

"Boy, I wish I could wake up like that."

"Hi, Milo. That's a cool haircut."

"No, I woke up like this, José."

"Yes, that looks really nice."

"Thanks, Ethan."

"Thanks, Xavia and Kayla."

"Hi, Milo. I love your hair."

"Hey, Milo. That's a stupid-looking haircut," said Dave. "Yeah, I said it! Your haircut looks stupid!"

"Come on, Milo; keep walking. He's a bully; just ignore him," said José.

"Mr. Milo, you look handsome today," Mrs. Barclay remarked.

"Thank you, Mrs. Barclay. So you don't think it's stupid?"

"Of course not, Milo. It's a sporty haircut. I'm sure my son would like a haircut like that, and everybody else would also."

Milo smile d and mumbled with a sad look, "Well, not everyone."

Well, not everyone.

9

"Dad,, will you take me to the barbershop to see Uncle Mac today?"

"Sure son, —is everything all right?"

"Yes, but not really."

"Son, is there any way I can help?"

"Dad, you're always there for me. I just need to speak with Uncle Mac today."

"All right, son, but afterward, we're going to get milkshakes."

"Great! I'd love that."

"Hi, Uncle Mac."

"Hey, what's with the long face?"

"Well, this boy named Dave called my haircut ugly and stupid. So can you change it back?"

11

"Why don't you hop up in my chair, shorty, so we can talk a bit? Let me guess— the kids at school were telling you they liked your haircut."

"Yes! How did you know, Uncle Mac?"

"Shorty, I've been cutting hair since long before you were born.

"Son, kids can be bullies sometimes because they see others do the same thing. That's what they learn. Bullies are miserable people, and they want you to be miserable too.

"How did it make you feel when that kid called your haircut ugly and stupid?"

"I was sad, and I didn't want the haircut anymore."

"Exactly! Weren't you happy before he said that?"

"Yes, I was Uncle Mac."

"Bullies are people who can change your positive attitude to a negative attitude if you let them.

"Bullies say mean things to you, and they want you to say mean things back to them.

"If you do that, it means you're a bully too, and you're just like them."

"But I didn't do anything to him ! My friend even told me to keep walking."

"Son, bullies don't need a reason to hurt other people's feelings. If the other kids were telling you they liked your haircut, did it ever dawn on you to think that he wanted someone to like his haircut too or be his friend?"

"No, I didn't think about that. I just kept walking with my friend."

"Well, you did the right thing, but sometimes you have to speak up for yourself. So the next time someone says mean words to you, follow the Golden Rule."

"What Golden Rule, Uncle Mac?"

"Treat others the way you want to be treated."

"So I should say something nice to that person so my positive attitude won't turn into a bad attitude."

"That's correct, son."

BE KIND

"You always treat others with respect. No one should be calling people mean names, teasing, hitting, or laughing at others. This is not how people should treat each other, and this is not how you were raised."

"I understand ."

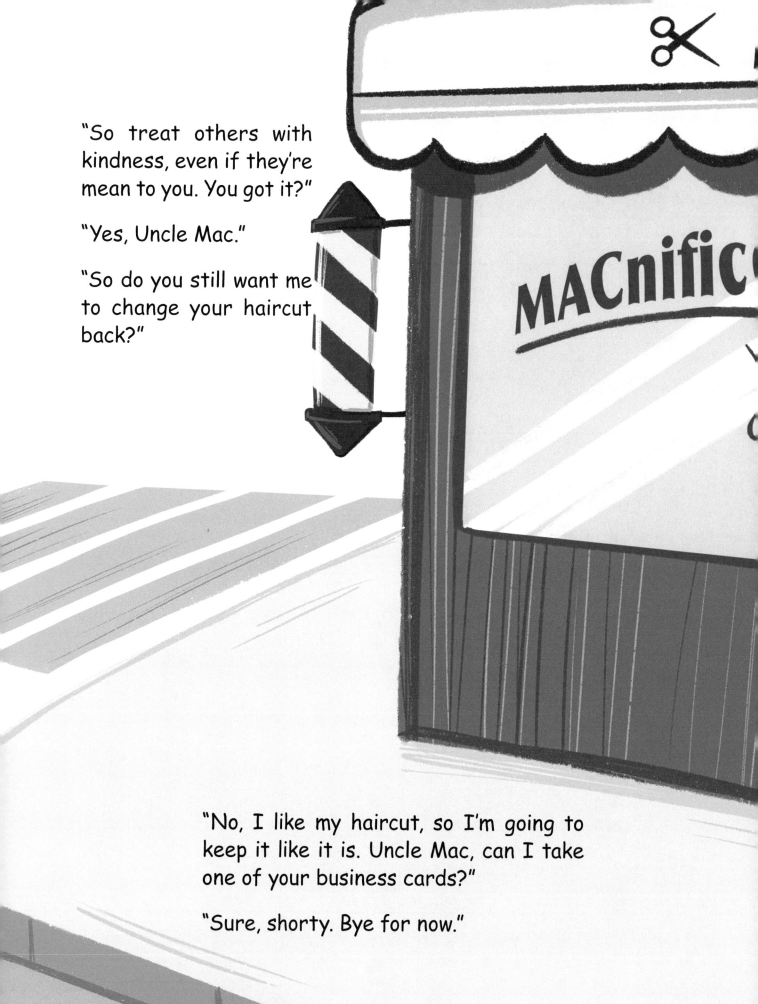

"So treat others with kindness, even if they're mean to you. You got it?"

"Yes, Uncle Mac."

"So do you still want me to change your haircut back?"

"No, I like my haircut, so I'm going to keep it like it is. Uncle Mac, can I take one of your business cards?"

"Sure, shorty. Bye for now."

"What's up, ugly- face hairdo?"

"Hi, Dave. It's not nice to say mean things to people."

"What did you say to me, Milo?"

Milo looked at Dave and said with a shaky voice, "I'm just saying— if you don't like my haircut, there's no need to say it's ugly because that's mean."

"Well, it's ugly, and it's stupid!"

"You know what, Dave? I like my haircut, and I think it's cool."

"Come on, Milo; let's go," said José.

Milo replied, "Go ahead, José. I'll see you in class."

Then he turned to Dave and said, "I'm not going to say mean things back to you just because you say them to me. That's not how people should treat each other."

Dave replied, "You don't know me, so don't tell me how to treat others."

"You're right, Dave. I don't know you, but would you like to get a pretty cool haircut too? My uncle Mac can put any design in your hair; plus, he has a lot of cool kids' designs."

Dave looked shocked and replied, "Well, yeah, I guess I'd like that."

"I like soccer; can he put a soccer ball design in my hair?" asked Dave.

"He sure can," said Milo. "Here's the address to his barbershop."

"Uh, well, thanks."

"You're welcome, Dave. Bye for now."

"Hi, Dave; that's a cool haircut."

"Yes, that looks really nice."

"Hi, Dave! I love your hair."

25

"Hey, Dave, did you get a new haircut?"

"Yes, José."

"Thanks, Ethan."

"Thanks, Xavia and Kayla."

Dave approached Milo and José . "Hi, Milo, " said Dave.

"Nice haircut!"

"Yeah, thanks. I wanted to say I'm sorry for calling your haircut ugly and stupid. I didn't realize my words hurt people's feelings until Uncle Mac talked to me while cutting my hair.

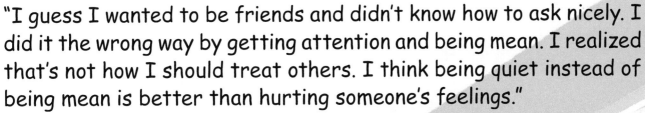

"I guess I wanted to be friends and didn't know how to ask nicely. I did it the wrong way by getting attention and being mean. I realized that's not how I should treat others. I think being quiet instead of being mean is better than hurting someone's feelings."

28

"Will you accept my apology, and will you be my friend?"

"Of course," replied Milo.

"I'll be your friend too, Dave," said José.

"Thanks, guys, I'd like that! Now, who wants to play soccer after school?"

Word List

A — Apology   N — Nod

B — Barbershop   O — Other

C — Course   P — Pancakes

D — Dawn   Q — Quiet

E — Exactly   R — Reason

F — Football   S — Soccer

G — Guess   T — Treat

H — Haircut   U — Uncle

I — Ignore   V — Voice

J — José   W — Wake

K — Kind   X — Xavia

L — Laughing   Y — Yeah

M — Magnificent   Z — Zigzag

Connect with the Characters

How did Dave behave like a bully?	Have you ever been bullied? If so, what happened, and how did you handle the situation?
How did Milo get Dave to stop bullying him?	What advice did Uncle Mac give Milo to handle the bullying situation? Did Milo use the advice or not?
Explain why Jose told Milo to keep walking when he saw what was happening?	What advice would you give Milo about the bullying situation?
If you could draw a picture of a Stop Bullying sign, what would it look like?	Do you have someone in your life like Uncle Mac who gives you good advice? If so, who is it?

Join us for story time and Eventbrite.com events with your book purchase.
Search for "Sip and Read *Uncle Mac's Barbershop: A Lesson about Bullying.*"

Website: Drfigueroa1913.com
Email: Drfigueroa1913@gmail.com

Printed in the United States
by Baker & Taylor Publisher Services